The
Climate
Diet

Also by Paul Greenberg

The Omega Principle

American Catch

Four Fish

The
Climate
Diet

50 Simple Ways to Trim
Your Carbon Footprint

Paul Greenberg

PENGUIN BOOKS

PENGUIN BOOKS
An imprint of Penguin Random House LLC
penguinrandomhouse.com

LIBRARY OF CONGRESS CATALOGING-IN-PUBLICATION DATA
Name: Greenberg, Paul, 1967– author.
Title: The climate diet : 50 simple ways to trim
your carbon footprint / Paul Greenberg.
Description: New York : Penguin Books, 2021. |
Includes bibliographical references.
Identifiers: LCCN 2020037520 (print) | LCCN 2020037521 (ebook) |
ISBN 9780593296769 (trade paperback) | ISBN 9780593296776 (ebook)
Subjects: LCSH: Food--Environmental aspects. | Carbon dioxide mitigation.
Classification: LCC TX357 .G74 2021 (print) |
LCC TX357 (ebook) | DDC 613.2—dc23
LC record available at https://lccn.loc.gov/2020037520
LC ebook record available at https://lccn.loc.gov/2020037521

Printed in the United States of America
1st Printing

Set in Adobe Garamond Pro
Designed by Alexis Farabaugh

Paul Greenberg is available for select speaking engagements. To inquire about
a possible appearance, please contact Penguin Random House Speakers
Bureau at speakers@penguinrandomhouse.com or visit prhspeakers.com.

Nothing shall come of nothing.

—William Shakespeare, *King Lear*

Contents

Introduction:
Nothing or Something?

Should we do nothing or should we do something?

There's a lot we can ask ourselves about climate change, but in the end, this is the question that
really matters in the immediate experience of living
our lives. Should we put our very own shoulders to
the wheel before us, grinding out, through our own
efforts, a transformation of our culture, our economy and, really, life as we know it, or should we lie
down before this rising sea of troubles, accept the
futility of opposing them, and hope that we some-
how survive in what is rapidly becoming a less and
less livable world? Do we give up on economically

disadvantaged communities that have already been disproportionately punished by choking heat and devastating floods? Do we abandon the hope that our children and grandchildren will live lives free from the famine and civil strife that current models forecast for us in the overheated decades ahead?

If you've picked up this book, you're probably of the "do something" variety. You are of a mind to take stock of your life, even if your life to date has not been particularly green. Or perhaps you have already done a thing or two to turn your behavior in a more climate-friendly direction, but are not quite sure if those changes are meaningful. Maybe you are a parent or grandparent who has just been on the receiving end of "the speech" from a teen or twentysomething about how the boomers and Gen Xers have set their descendants up for disaster. Maybe you're wondering if there are a couple of reasonable things you could do to keep the peace with that young person in your life. Or maybe you yourself are that teen or twentysomething coming into adulthood and wondering how you can win over hearts and minds to climate action within your family and your community. In any of these cases, I think the pages that follow can help.

Introduction: Nothing or Something?

This book came about because I wanted to address an essential disconnect that keeps many Americans on the sidelines of climate action. On the one hand, awareness of the problem has risen markedly in the last few years and many more Americans want to do something to fix it. On the other hand, most scientists and policy makers have correctly identified the crisis as far bigger than the scope of what one person can do. Both perspectives are valid. But when they collide, the psychological effect on the average citizen is paralysis. "Where is my place in all this?" a person confronted with this dilemma wonders. "What can I possibly do that is meaningful?"

This paralysis is particularly evident here in the United States. For when you dive down into the numbers, America stands out starkly as a place that is profoundly stuck.

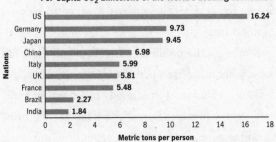

Per Capita CO$_2$ Emissions of the World's Leading Economies

Nations	Metric tons per person
US	16.24
Germany	9.73
Japan	9.45
China	6.98
Italy	5.99
UK	5.81
France	5.48
Brazil	2.27
India	1.84

Introduction: Nothing or Something?

Presently the United States is, per capita, by far the most prodigious emitter of carbon dioxide among the world's leading economic powers, with a carbon footprint of around 16 metric tons of CO_2 per person per year. This is all the more troubling when we compare where we are versus where we need to get. The UN suggests a global target for per capita emissions of a little over 3 tons. India at 1.8 tons of CO_2 per person is already there. One could argue that this is only the case because India lacks the industrial infrastructure of more developed nations. But many economic powerhouses show that advanced development and low emissions are not incompatible. France, the UK, and Italy all have per capita emissions around a third of what the United States puts into the atmosphere. China handily bests us as well. Two citizens of the People's Republic emit less CO_2 than a single American. There is no way to avoid it: the world desperately needs America to go on a climate diet.

But here's the problem: most diets fail. They fail mostly because after a period of bingeing, we set unrealistic goals for reforming our bad ways. In time, self-control breaks down and we hunger to throw open the cupboards and binge again.

Still, some diets *do* work. Those successful diets tend to be modest in their goals, incorporating small changes over long periods of time. That we need to transform the very roots of the American economy is without doubt and something that must be fought for intensely. But not every well-meaning American will engage in a protracted political struggle. Not all of us are Dr. Seuss's raging Loraxes, who "speak for the trees." While we might not want to admit it, most of us are go-about-our-business Seussian Whos.

Fortunately, there are smaller maintainable changes that would allow American Whos to go from carbon obese to just a little bit carbon overweight. And, in the end, the transformation of that sizeable carbon-obese American middle to a modest paunch would do more for reducing total global emissions than if a hyper-virtuous 2 percent came to subsist on lentils and solar panels.

To shrink that middle, we need to find climate actions that can be taken up by both coasts *and* the heartland. And there's evidence to suggest that this is politically tenable. A 2019 Reuters/Ipsos poll showed that a significant majority of Americans believe in the necessity of taking action to fight climate change, irrespective of political affiliation. The challenge lies in getting that majority to actually take action rather than just want action to be taken. So part of this book's intent is to propose realistic actions that will get as many hands on deck as possible.

At the same time, our diet can't be so modest that it amounts to only a cosmetic tweaking. We *do* need radical transformation, as individuals and as a society. We therefore need to make personal changes that have a multiplier effect: changes that beget more change. Swapping out incandescent lightbulbs for LEDs will trim a few pounds off your annual emissions. But changing the actual *source* of the electricity running to your home will start to shift the entire energy economy away from fossil fuels and toward a lower emissions future. The first four chapters of this book offer practical guidance on making changes on that scale.

But personal behavior change is only one part of the battle. At this critical juncture, all of us need to find our inner Lorax. We need to speak truth to money and power, even if some of our voices might have less volume than others. And so the last two chapters of this book lay out a blueprint for how we can act to affect the climate policies of businesses and government.

While I had to make judgment calls as to which rules to include in this short guide, the behavior change suggestions themselves came from seasoned researchers and practitioners from an array of different disciplines: agronomists, energy efficiency experts, urban planners, foresters, financial advisors, political activists, and lawmakers. Within each chapter, I have tried to list the actions individuals can take from easiest to most ambitious. I know, for example, that most car-owning Americans don't have the resources to ditch their fossil fuel–burning vehicle and buy a new Tesla. But *anyone* can bring the pressure in their tires to the most fuel-efficient level. If we all did that, we would cut American gasoline consumption by anywhere from 2 to 8 percent. Not only that, we'd walk away from that change with a few more dollars in our pockets. Which brings me to the other necessary criterion for a climate rule to be ranked number one or two: each of the top two actions within each chapter should not cost you anything—and, in most cases, will save you money in the short and long term.

This is not a "gotcha" book; for who in this world can avoid "getting got" for their climate transgressions? Rather, this is a book meant to help you get from wherever you are right now to a better place in the future. If you were to change your ways in compliance with only the ones and twos in each chapter, you would already be doing this country and this planet some good. But if you come to this book having already tackled ones and twos, why not consider the threes, the fours, and, dare I say it, the fives, sixes and sevens? Most of the suggestions do not require large outlays of cash. Nor are any of them tremendous time burdens. Mostly what they require is a consistent mindfulness with respect to climate: a daily awareness of the crisis at hand and a daily response to that crisis.

All of the items contained within this book emphasize actions, not words. For talk, truly, is cheap and nowadays more often than not just a prelude to an unproductive partisan argument. To see around the corner of despair and glimpse hope, we all need to do something. Only by actually doing something can we gain that perspective.

Here, then, are fifty ideas for doing something instead of nothing.

The
Climate
Diet

Eating and Drinking

We make choices about food more often than about any other climate change driver. It therefore makes sense to begin our climate diet with our actual diet. Though it is a complicated business assigning an overall number to the carbon footprint of food, most regulators and scientists place it within the top five sources of emissions, nationally. These emissions happen directly through the operation of farm equipment, the methane burps of cows, and the transportation of product to market, and also indirectly through the replacement of powerful carbon-sequestering wild systems like forests and grasslands with CO_2-leaking monocultures like corn and wheat. Even the earth beneath our feet is diminished by present methods of agriculture. The global soil stock, the world's second largest carbon storehouse after the ocean, has lost somewhere between 50 and 70 percent of its original carbon dioxide to the atmosphere because of overtilling, overfertilization, excessive pesticide application, and other practices commonly deployed in the modern food system.

There are other important reasons to focus on fixing your food footprint. Biodiversity, water use, and exploitation of open space—key metrics in how scientists assess sustainability—are all profoundly impacted by how we grow our food. The central issue of this book, though, is greenhouse gas emissions, so I've organized this chapter around which food changes would have the largest impact on that metric. With apologies to the animal liberation movement (which I support), the approach here is not specifically vegan or vegetarian but rather what some call "climatarian"— an emphasis on the most realistic food changes that could be taken up by the largest number of people to lop the greatest possible chunk off American emissions. Here, then, is a baker's dozen of changes you can make that will lighten your emissions load in the kitchen.

1

Ease up on meat and cheese. A switch to a plant-based diet shaves at least a ton of CO_2 per year off your carbon footprint. But even just eating fewer pounds of animal products can be highly impactful. Beef can cost the planet more than 27 kilograms of CO_2 emissions per kilogram of meat. The emissions cost of producing beef is consistently high regardless of how cattle are raised. Both ham and cheese are also emissions-intense—each of them comes in at more than 11 kilograms of CO_2 per kilogram of food. Some might fret that eating fewer animal products would cause a protein deficit. Untrue. Americans actually overeat protein by about 30 percent. In spite of what fad diets might tell you, the USDA recommends only about 90 grams per day for men and 60 grams for women—less than one McDonald's small hamburger. And unlike carbohydrates or fats, excess protein can't be stored in the body—we literally piss it away.

The Climate Diet

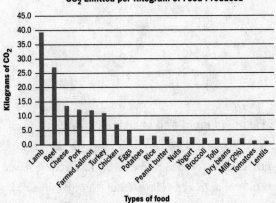

CO_2 Emitted per Kilogram of Food Produced

Types of food

2

Consider the chicken. Once you've reduced your overall intake of animal products, choose the kinds of protein you do eat with emissions in mind. At less than 7 kilograms of CO_2 per kilogram of meat, chicken ranks as the most emissions-efficient widely produced terrestrial animal protein. True, it's no lentil—it takes a minuscule .9 kilograms of CO_2 for a kilogram of that little brown bean to come to market. But if every beef-eating American switched to chicken, the United States would cut its carbon emissions by over 200 million tons.

3

Or the fish. Wild fish can be even more carbon efficient than chicken. An average of all American wild-caught finfish comes in at 1.6 kilograms of emissions per kilogram of edible fish flesh. That's because wild fish don't require feed or husbandry to reach harvestable size. Nature takes care of that. The primary emissions cost of wild fish is the burden of catching them and transporting them to market. But not all wild fish are good emissions bargains. The word *fish* comprises thousands of species caught in dozens of different ways. Fishing methods that entail long journeys into distant waters with repeated stops to haul gear burn a lot of diesel. So, for instance, longline-caught tuna and swordfish sit near the top of the fisheries emissions list. Dragging heavy gear over the seafloor is also carbon-expensive, making flounder, cod, and other "bottom-trawled" species less desirable choices. Conversely, seafood that is caught in midwater trawls and purse seines—nets that don't touch the bottom—tend to be carbon lightest. Alaska pollock (the fish most commonly found in your Filet-O-Fish), and small pelagic fish like mackerel, sardines, herring, squid, and anchovies, all fall into this carbon-light category. Farmed fish, meanwhile, tend to float around in an emissions space somewhere between chicken and pork.

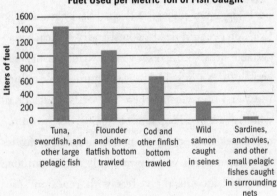

Fuel Used per Metric Ton of Fish Caught

Liters of fuel (y-axis: 0, 200, 400, 600, 800, 1000, 1200, 1400, 1600)

Types of fish:
- Tuna, swordfish, and other large pelagic fish
- Flounder and other flatfish bottom trawled
- Cod and other finfish bottom trawled
- Wild salmon caught in seines
- Sardines, anchovies, and other small pelagic fishes caught in surrounding nets

4

Make oysters your appetizer instead of shrimp.
All those shrimp cocktails add up: out of the 15
pounds of fish and shellfish Americans eat each year,
more than 4 pounds are shrimp, making shrimp by
far the most popular seafood in the United States.
But shrimp, particularly farmed shrimp, are notably
terrible from an emissions point of view—by some
estimates as bad as beef. That's in part because over
the last few decades, shrimp farming has destroyed
millions of acres of one of the world's most powerful
carbon-sequestering ecosystems: mangrove forests.
Mangroves, on average, store more than twice the CO_2
per acre as tropical rain forests but are often cleared
to make way for coastal shrimp ponds. All this makes
a shrimp cocktail an extremely carbon-intensive appetizer. Oysters, meanwhile, carry none of these
costs. In fact, farmed bivalves—oysters, clams, and
mussels—are extremely carbon-light. They require no
feed, subsisting on a diet of wild algae and filtering

and cleaning the water as they grow fat. That clever trick puts some bivalves in the same carbon cost range as many vegetables. Mussels, the grand emissions champions of the animal kingdom (and also one of the most affordable seafoods out there), can cost just .6 kilograms of carbon and other greenhouse gasses per kilogram of mussel meat. Take that, lentil!

5

Be a picky plant eater. It's undeniable that a good vegan diet can do more to cut a person's greenhouse gas emissions budget than any other kind of eating pattern. But as the environmental physicist Gidon Eshel puts it, "You can be a perfectly terrible citizen of the world and be vegan, or you can be a perfectly upstanding citizen of the world while eating animals. Both are possible." There are three main reasons for this. The first is the aforementioned point about protein. Overeating the protein component while on a vegan diet can unnecessarily add emissions pounds to what would otherwise be a green way of eating. The second problem can be food processing. Taking apart plant-based nutrients and reassembling them in such a way that makes them resemble animal products takes energy. True, the new wave of hyper-processed meat replacements (Beyond and Impossible burgers, for example) have about half the carbon footprint of chicken. But they are still about five times more emissions-intense than a simple bean patty. The third reason some plant-based diets can be problematic brings us to our next rule.

6

Be thoughtful with local. The food movement of the last twenty years has stressed the importance of sourcing food from local producers, and we've seen a tremendous proliferation of farmers' markets as a result. Buying locally does keep family farms working and saves land from real estate development, which can in and of itself be good for emissions reductions. But local farming can be carbon intensive. In an effort to meet supermarket-style everything-always demand, some small-scale farmers have adopted practices to grow crops that don't naturally prosper where their farms happen to be located. Take a wintertime salad. Growing greens in cold months in the Northeast requires heated greenhouses and other carbon-intensive practices. It is therefore much more carbon-efficient to get those same winter greens from California, where higher ambient temperatures and economies of scale mean that the overall carbon inputs are much lower, even when you include transport cost (about 10 percent of most food's carbon burden). If you still want to eat Northeastern greens in the Northeast in cold months, think about something that's regionally and seasonally appropriate, like cabbage. Be thoughtful and strategic when you drive to the farmers' market as well. Emissions-wise, a 20-mile round trip to buy a single head of broccoli is notably wasteful.

7

Roots rule. In case you're wondering which foods deliver the absolute most nutrients for the absolute least emissions, the answer according to the most recent comparative analyses is . . . carrots. Sorry not to be more exciting, but roots like carrots and parsnips carry with them a strikingly low emissions cost. The second best performer in terms of nutrients delivered per unit of carbon dioxide emitted is . . . sorry, again, not so exciting: small pelagic wild fish like anchovies. Little fish also rule.

8

Avoid flying food. By flying food, I mean air-freighted food. While a more hospitable, distant climate can offset the carbon cost of transporting food when the transport mode is ship or rail, airfreighting is so emissions-expensive that it blows away any other consideration. Overall, air-freighting food is fifty times more carbon costly than the least carbon intensive, transporting by ship. Flying foods are typically highly perishable products brought to us at great speed to avoid spoilage. Since fuel efficiency declines the faster you go, this is a decidedly wasteful practice. One study in the UK found that while only 1.5 percent of fruit and vegetables in that country are carried by air, they accounted for 40 percent of the total CO_2 used in transport of produce for the entire nation. Flying food is almost never labeled as such in the marketplace, so a good rule of thumb is to avoid nonlocal fresh fish as well as highly perishable fruits and vegetables like berries, pineapples, asparagus, and green beans when they are out of season.

9

Make friends with frozen. Because frozen food can be transported slowly over longer periods of time, it is more likely to be sent via ship, which is by far the most carbon efficient way of getting food to our plates. In addition, frozen foods typically have as much nutritional value as fresh foods and, in some cases, when fresh food has been sitting on the shelf for extended periods of time, even more. Lastly, frozen foods are often cheaper.

10

Buy your food naked. Overall, packaging accounts for around 5 percent of food's carbon footprint. If you must buy packaged food, reuse that packaging whenever possible to store food at home. You can also consider recyclable beeswax wrapping—a material that can be washed and reused hundreds of times—to store food. Be particularly mindful of aluminum foil. Aluminum manufacture requires a tremendous amount of electricity—around 3 percent of the global supply, resulting in 1 percent of all the world's greenhouse gas emissions. Buy it in recycled form, clean it when you're done, and use it again (and, if possible, again and again).

11

Fix your waste management. Americans throw out about 40 percent of their food. This is an egregious addition to our carbon footprint, not to mention hugely wasteful in general. But wasted food has another pernicious climate effect. Food waste in landfills, starved of oxygen, releases methane, which has a warming consequence dozens of times that of CO_2. Because of food waste, the United States has larger landfill emissions than any other country on Earth, the equivalent of 37 million cars on the road each year. You should therefore think about the entire life cycle of your food before you buy it. Look at the available space in your refrigerator and freezer before going shopping. Plan weekly meals with an eye toward moving perishables from fridge to freezer as they approach their expiration dates. Once everything has been used to its fullest extent, compost what's left. A home composting bin is easy to build or inexpensive to buy. You can even make one that works in an apartment (see the Resources section at the end of this book for a guide). If you don't have access to composting space, see if your town or city has a composting program. If it doesn't, encourage your elected officials to start one.

12

Cook smarter. Cooking accounts for 4.5 percent of household energy use—not a lot, but worth addressing as it's a fairly easy fix. Putting lids on your pots when you boil water, for example, cuts cooking time (and energy use) in half. Soaking not just beans but also pasta in advance of cooking is similarly effective in reducing energy consumption. More ambitiously, you could consider replacing your gas stovetop with an electric one. Gas poses many climate problems— which I'll discuss in further detail in the "Staying Home" chapter—but the most glaring one is that when you cook on a gas stove, only about 40 percent of the energy from the flame gets to your food. Since gas ranges are responsible for the majority of the toxic nitrogen oxides that end up trapped in your home, switching to electric also has significant health benefits. Induction electric stovetops, which conduct 80 to 90 percent of cooking energy into your food, can cost under $150 for a simple plug-in, two-burner model.

13

Drink from the tap. Tap water is by far the cheapest drink we can consume in terms of both emissions and money. Nevertheless, the average American drinks about 42 gallons of bottled water every year—spending about $18 billion annually or something like $50 per person annually. A 2007 study found that making the billions of plastic bottles manufactured every year to hold all of that water used the equivalent of around 17 million barrels of oil—enough energy to fuel more than a million American cars and light trucks for a year. Yes, contamination of the American public water system is a serious problem, and we need to fight for clean, safe drinking water for all. But 90 percent of Americans have access to clean water 365 days a year. For some of the remaining 10 percent, an inexpensive water filter can address the problem (see the Resources section at the end of this book for a guide).

Making Families

I t's a painful truth: the single most powerful way Americans can reduce their carbon footprint is by creating fewer Americans. A child born today in the United States will generate 16 tons of CO_2 per year for the rest of their life and, in turn, that child will have their own 16-tons-per-person children, and so on. At the same time, when asked what makes their lives most meaningful, a substantial portion of Americans will say family. How can we reconcile the fact that establishing a multi-child household in a developed nation compromises our future with the fact that family ties are often what make our present lives worth living? We can start by addressing how we behave in our existing family configurations and think more carefully about how we add people to the planet.

14

Don't emit when you gather. Any large gathering where family members are called in from great distances can incur huge carbon costs. Figure at least 1 ton of carbon per domestic fly-in guest, 2 tons per international attendee. Changing the pattern of your family gatherings with respect to flying might be the easiest behavior you can modify. You can start with your wedding. Consider choosing a wedding location that is proximate to the majority of attendees. If you must have fly-in guests, suggest they take direct flights when possible, since takeoffs and landings account for 25 percent of a flight's emissions. Climate consciousness should be a part of all major events in your life from birth to death. Why not plan to plant a tree instead of a tombstone to mark your passing. Unlike an engraved piece of rock that will fade before your grandchildren die, a tree can keep growing and storing carbon for many future generations.

15

Reimagine gifts. Making and shipping new things burns fuel. And then there's the packaging. About a billion trees are cut down every year to make the boxes for Amazon and other online retailers. If we continue apace with online gifts for two more decades as we did over the last two, the equivalent of 5 percent of the trees of the actual Amazon will have been cut down for boxes. Instead of impulse purchasing online, consider giving homemade gifts. If you have more money to spend, give a tree planted in the recipient's honor. If someone is saving for higher education, contributions to a college fund are emissions-free. You could also consider the symbolic gift of a carbon offset, a credit for greenhouse gas reductions achieved by one party that can be purchased and used to compensate the emissions of another party; think of it as donating to a charity in someone's honor. A guide to carbon-free gifting is included in the Resources section.

16

Carnivorous pets have big carbon pawprints.
A midsize dog—a collie, golden retriever, or
Labrador—carries 19 percent of the energy requirements of a human. Cats are energy intensive as well,
although less so on account of their smaller size. Vegetarian birds, reptiles, and rodents like guinea pigs or
hamsters are substantially less carbon-costly than
either dogs or cats.

17

Make a different kind of family plan. Around two children per family (2.1 actually) is the "replacement value" for a stable human US population. But going beyond just stabilizing America's population and instead actually reducing it would be the most powerful way of stabilizing our climate. So take a very serious pause when you consider having multiple children. Some worry about the socialization problems only children may face. There are many ways to address these concerns: single-child family affiliations, community groups, and joint vacation planning can help alleviate only-child loneliness (see the Resources section at the end of this book). Adopting and fostering children can also be considered. Other, more unorthodox models exist. Some parents, particularly in the LGBTQ community, choose to pair up with a second couple and share child-raising responsibilities four ways. Still others find parenting satisfaction by mentoring children in their community. While considering family plans in the context of the environment may feel strange, think of it as of one piece of the effort to make Earth a livable place for all children in the future.

Staying Home

S ome of us rent, some of us own, but all of us can do better to improve the climate impacts of our homes. Because of dramatic advances made in renewable energy generation and energy-efficient appliances, options for reducing your at-home carbon footprint are often both affordable and relatively easy to deploy. If we had a government like Denmark's that set (and is on track to achieve!) an ambitious national goal of operating on 30 percent renewable power by the beginning of the present decade, we could sit back and let regulations bring us to a better place. But in the United States we consumers need to take a more active role in driving demand. The more we choose green energy solutions in our daily domestic lives, the more building and designing carbon-light will become the default for the residences of the future.

18

Change the grid if you can't get off it. For the green-economy fantasist, the idea of going "off grid" floats out there as a beautiful dream that never quite comes true. Entirely decoupling a home from the national energy network and building a stand-alone solar or wind generation system often ends up being too expensive and too daunting. But today, with more and more renewable energy being incorporated into the national energy grid it is possible to shop for better power options and route them through the old-style grid without having to lift a screwdriver or spend extra money. Why can working with the old grid be a good thing? Supply follows demand. If as many of us as possible demand renewable energy, economies of scale will start to lower renewable costs, and the grid itself will begin tilting away from fossil fuels and toward solar and wind. This is already happening to some extent, but we can accelerate the process by choosing to buy into renewables right now. To convert your energy supply from fossil fuel based to renewable, you will need to contract with what is called an energy service company, or ESCO. ESCOs will route your desired power option to your home, usually for a price comparable to your current electricity plan. For a step-by-step guide for contracting with an ESCO, see the resources section at the back of this book.

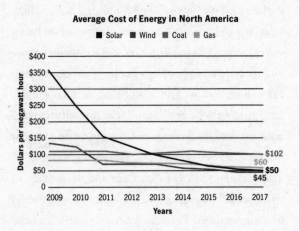

Average Cost of Energy in North America
■ Solar ■ Wind ■ Coal ▒ Gas

19

Buy power locally. You can take the decarbonizing of your electricity supply even further by sourcing at least some of your power from a community solar program. Community solar programs are neighborhood-based initiatives that fund the construction of local solar power plants for use by multiple homeowners. Think of it as the electricity equivalent of a community-supported agriculture program where you buy a share of produce from a local farm. Just as those programs help citizens grow local agriculture, community solar allows communities to build capacity for local power generation. Thirty-nine states now have community solar programs. As with an ESCO, you can shop online for providers and request that community solar be integrated into your electricity supply. Some of the most progressive states—New York, New Jersey, Colorado, and Maine—actually subsidize community solar so it can end up being cheaper for you.

20

Electrify. Once you've changed the source of the power coming into your home, you've opened up a whole new pathway to footprint shrinking: converting appliances from gas or oil to electric. This is an important step not only because new electrical appliances are often more efficient than gas ones, but also because natural gas, which has of late been sold to consumers as a cheaper and cleaner alternative, turns out to be invisibly problematic. Put simply, natural gas is leaky. Every time you turn on your stove, or every time your water heater fires up, methane leaks into the atmosphere. And before it even gets to your home, gas leaks from the ground during extraction and spurts out of pipelines as it moves from the gas field to home. What's more, natural gas is cheap now because a large customer base offsets the cost of its maintenance and expansion. But as renewables drop in price (as they markedly have in the last ten years), more and more customers will almost certainly switch to electric; those that remain on gas will bear larger individual costs to support a vast and expensive natural gas infrastructure.

21

Take control of your climate. The biggest emissions culprit in your home by far is your heating and air conditioning, making up around 60 percent of home energy use. If you have an industry-standard oil or gas furnace, the easiest way to shrink this piece of the pie is to turn down your thermostat at night. If you live in a colder northern state, just a 1-degree reduction in temperature will save your household about 40 kilograms of carbon emissions per year. But if you want to *really* shrink the heating and cooling part of your emissions, consider installing a relatively new electric-powered technology called a heat pump. Heat pumps save energy by moving heat instead of generating it (see the Resources section of this book for more details). Because they move heat from outdoors to indoors and indoors to outdoors, they can both heat and cool your home. True, heat pumps can be pricey—between $5,000 and $10,000 in most cases. However, the annual fuel savings can range from $500 to $1,000—enough over a decade of ownership to offset the up-front cost.

US Household Energy Use, 2019

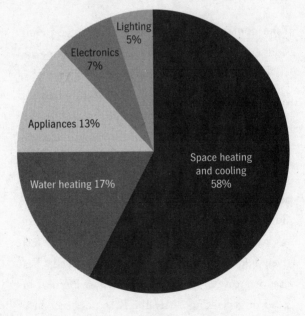

22

Educate your thermostat. Adding a low-cost programmable thermostat to your home takes smart heating and cooling to a new level. These low-cost devices turn your heating or cooling system on when you are usually home and off when you're away. They further enable you to create sophisticated schedules for every day of the week, anticipating your energy needs without your having to think about them. (Note: not all homes have the correct voltage to support this device, so homeowners and renters should read more about installing smart thermostats in the Resources section of this book.)

23

Fix the rest. The other major consumers of power in your home after heating and cooling are water heaters, clothes dryers, and stovetops. Efficient electric versions of all of these appliances are now readily available. As with a heat pump, the up-front cost of energy-efficient appliances can be significant, but over time, each efficient replacement will save you money in overall cost of operation.

24

Kill the vampire. In recent years, manufacturers have added standby modes to electronic devices, a feature that enables them to power up quickly. While this may be convenient for the consumer, it can be incredibly wasteful in terms of both energy and money. Standby power—also known as "vampire" power—adds up to 4.6 percent of America's annual residential CO_2 emissions, costing consumers on average $165 a year. Televisions, computers, and game consoles are the biggest offenders. Though it may take a few minutes here and there, you can put a stake in the vampire by fully powering down electronics at the end of the day or during any lengthy break between uses. Using power strips that allow you to turn off multiple devices at the same time will make the process of powering up and down more time efficient.

25

Dress carbon-light. The fashion industry is responsible for 10 percent of annual global carbon emissions, more than all international flights and maritime shipping combined, according to the World Bank. There are notable differences in emissions burdens of different fabric types—5.5 kilograms of emissions for a polyester shirt versus 4.3 for a cotton one. But lest you automatically choose the cotton over the synthetic, it's worth noting that one cotton shirt drinks up 2,700 liters of water—more than what one person drinks in two and a half years. Given the different overlapping problems of clothing manufacture, by far the best choice you can make with clothes is to use them longer and treat them better. Drying clothes in a dryer not only increases wear and tear, but dryers are the second most energy-intensive appliance in your home (after water heaters). So if you've got the time and the space, line-dry clothes whenever possible. When replacing clothes, look to thrift stores first.

26

Turn your backyard into a sink. Reducing the amount of CO_2 each of us puts into the atmosphere is only one part of solving the climate problem. We also need more of what climate scientists call carbon sinks—systems that *remove* CO_2 that's already found its way into the atmosphere. Engineers have proposed an array of human-made inventions to store carbon dioxide in the future, but the most powerful and readily expandable sinks are forests. In 2019, researchers wrote in the journal *Science* that more than 2 billion acres are available on the planet for reforestation. Once mature, these new forests could store 205 billion tons of carbon, or about 25 percent of the CO_2 currently in the atmosphere. American homeowners could do their part by turning some of their lawn space into tree space. Currently 40 million acres of American land is in lawn—indeed, grass is today the largest irrigated "crop" in the United

States. Because lawns sequester much less CO_2 than forest, transforming lawn space into tree space would do the planet a tremendous service. Just half an acre of lawn converted to forest and allowed to grow to maturity will sequester more CO_2 than a car emits in a year.

27

Live close. In the wake of the COVID-19 pandemic, those of you who live in the city may have been considering packing up and moving to a suburban or rural retreat. You might even think that this would make for greener living, allowing you to more directly control how you spend your energy budget. Not really. Living in a freestanding house and driving are so emissions-expensive that they overwhelm whatever reductions you might achieve by having more direct control over your day-to-day environment. So, think twice before you swap your city apartment for a place in the country. If you decide to relocate anyway, choose a home where you can easily walk or bike to public transportation.

Leaving Home

The space between home and the rest of the world is the hole into which we pour most of our emissions. According to the Brookings Institution, 76 percent of Americans drive to work alone every working day. All told, commuting to work represents around 17 percent of all the emissions we generate—and indeed, commuting is the main reason most Americans own a car in the first place. The impact can be even worse when we choose to travel by airplane. Here, then, are a few thoughts on ways we can trim our trips and travel more efficiently.

US Transportation Emissions by Vehicle Type, 2018

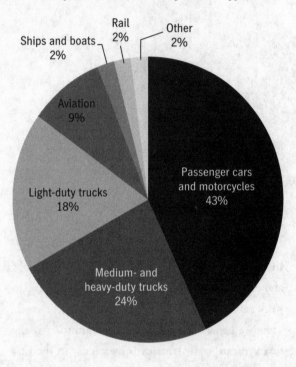

28

Trade a flying vacation for a better home. With the end of the COVID-19 pandemic possibly in sight as of this writing, many are eager to resume international travel. But a return to business-as-usual jet-setting will do much to afflict the climate. Just one round-trip flight from New York to London emits around 1 ton of CO_2 per person (other pollutants a jet puts into the upper atmosphere contribute mightily to the greenhouse effect, too). That's the CO_2 output of many individuals in the developing world for an entire year. In fact, a 2018 study in the journal *Nature* revealed that tourism accounts for about 8 percent of global greenhouse gas emissions. This all adds up in terms of money, too. Why not choose a non-flying vacation this year and use the money saved for a better home for years to come? Many of the suggestions in the previous section on home improvement can be accomplished for the same price as flying a family of four abroad.

29

If you own a car, make it a better commuter. If you're a car owner, ensure your vehicle is performing as fuel efficiently as possible. Inflate your tires to the manufacturer's recommended pressure. Correctly inflated tires can improve your mileage from 2 to 8 percent. Keeping your car tuned up can get you another 4 percent improvement in mileage. Ensuring that you're using your carmaker's recommended oil weight can buy 2 percent more. Once you've made these mechanical fixes, fix your driving behavior with an eye toward fuel efficiency. Aggressive accelerating and braking and over-the-speed-limit driving decrease your fuel efficiency. When you get to your destination, turn off the engine. Engine idling accounts for 1.6 percent of all carbon dioxide emissions in the United States every year. And of course the most efficient way to use your car is not to use it at all. Public transport or, better yet, cycling and walking markedly outperform even the most efficient use of a gasoline-powered car.

30

Keep the telecommuting habit. If you were lucky enough to be able to work remotely during the COVID-19 crisis and have since returned to work post-COVID, it's worth asking your employer: Why? A rigorous two-year Stanford University study found that employees who switched to telecommuting ended up squeezing close to a full extra day of labor out of the workweek. The stay-home employees in the study also outperformed the control group by taking fewer sick days, shorter breaks, and, of course, never being late. And while the study was conducted pre-COVID, during an earlier time when children stuck at home weren't distracting moms and dads working from home, it's worth noting the study concluded that businesses could save significant amounts of money by shrinking their office sizes. Perhaps some of those savings in the future might be directed to an employee childcare benefit for stay-at-home parents.

31

Question the conference. In the wake of the COVID crisis, most of the world's business conferences were canceled, resulting in millions of tons of emissions savings. If you are normally obligated to attend conferences as part of your work, strongly consider attending your next meeting digitally if such resources are available. If you happen to be in charge of scheduling conferences for your company or organization, consider making the next event virtual.

32

Business class is too expensive for the environment. A business class seat has a huge carbon price to accompany its large financial cost—two and a half to three times the emissions impact as a seat in economy. If you must travel for work, do your employer and the planet a favor and be low-class when you fly. Of course, the same rule applies for leisure travelers, too.

33

If you have to drive, drive electric. As I wrote at the top of this section, driving is America's number one climate problem. We drive too often and too inefficiently, and invest too much of our open space and infrastructure funding on our 4 million miles of roadways. Overall, we need fewer cars, more public transportation, and more land turned back over into carbon sinks like forests and grasslands.

All that being said, realistically speaking, we will not see the end of the American automobile anytime soon. It's for this and a few other reasons that I will make what I know to be, in some circles, a controversial pitch for converting the existing American car population to electric as soon as possible.

First of all, prices for electric vehicles get closer to those of gasoline-powered cars with each passing year. And since charging a car with electricity costs on average only about a buck per gallon-equivalent, the difference in up-front ownership cost between electric and gasoline-powered cars will be mostly if not entirely erased over the course of an electric vehicle's lifetime. All told, ten years of electric vehicle ownership is likely to save you around $9,000 in fuel costs.

Driving an electric vehicle also contributes in a key, albeit invisible, way to bolstering renewable energy. One of the biggest obstacles to expanding solar and wind energy is the difficulty we have in storing it. Storing electricity is expensive, requiring the construction of extensive battery arrays that most utility companies balk at funding. Since wind and solar generation are often at their peak at times when we can't use the power, storing it in some way is critical to making renewables more widespread. Electric vehicles are usually charged at night, when wind tends to blow the hardest, or at lunch time, when the sun shines with the greatest intensity. If we replace America's existing fossil fuel–powered cars and trucks with electric vehicles we will in effect create a nationwide battery grid capable of absorbing those inconveniently timed renewable energy spikes, storing that power for later use when people commute to and from work. This concept, known as vehicle-to-grid (V2G for green energy geeks), is something that is rapidly moving out of academic think tanks and into practical applications. If we replace more internal combustion engines with electric, we will speed the trend and further incentivize the construction of more wind and solar.

Saving and Spending

n September 2019, the author and climate activist Bill McKibben wrote an article in *The New Yorker* titled "Money Is the Oxygen on Which the Fire of Global Warming Burns." McKibben made the powerful case that changing the way we save, borrow, invest, and insure has a direct impact on whether or not that fire keeps burning. All of us are implicated in the fossil fuel economy through money. Our banks underwrite not only our credit cards, but also capital-intensive oil drilling projects in far-flung parts of the globe. Insurance companies cover not only the risks associated with owning or renting a home, but also the extreme peril fossil fuel companies face when they prospect under Arctic ice, drill beneath waters thousands of feet deep, or blow open

West Virginia mountaintops to get at the coal inside. Once again, US institutions lead the world in financing these emissions-costly activities. According to "Banking on Climate Change," an annual report compiled by the Rainforest Action Network, four out of the top five investment banks that have most increased their fossil fuel underwriting since the 2016 Paris Agreement are American. JPMorgan Chase, by far the largest fossil fuel investor in the world, leads the pack, followed by Wells Fargo, Citibank, and Bank of America. In your interactions with financial institutions, you have many opportunities to push for change. By directly questioning the underwriters of your credit cards and bank accounts you can raise awareness and effect change within financial institutions. If you are fortunate enough to have an investment portfolio, you can ensure that the stocks, bonds, and mutual funds you choose don't perpetuate the fossil fuel economy. And remember, climate change disproportionately affects economically disadvantaged communities, so wealthier individuals should feel doubly obligated to make their money do the greatest green good.

Saving and Spending

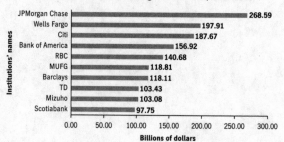

Financial Institutions' Financing of Fossil Fuels, 2016–2019

Institutions' names	Billions of dollars
JPMorgan Chase	268.59
Wells Fargo	197.91
Citi	187.67
Bank of America	156.92
RBC	140.68
MUFG	118.81
Barclays	118.11
TD	103.43
Mizuho	103.08
Scotiabank	97.75

34

Pressure your financial institutions to be better.
There are many ways to inform your financial institutions that you're not on board with fossil fuel underwriting. McKibben advises bluntly: "Cut up your Chase credit card." Other options include writing to or calling your branch manager, account representative, or corporate headquarters to indicate that your continued business depends on a plan to end the support of the fossil fuel industry. Increase your impact by collecting letters from your friends and colleagues applying the same pressure. Also, remember that convincing a large institution to divest from fossil fuels is a long-term effort. The students at Middlebury College, where McKibben teaches, fought for six years before the college agreed to divest. "The college's students never gave up, passing on the activist

torch to each new freshman class," McKibben wrote in *The Guardian*. Now the college has gone even further, pledging to cut energy consumption on campus by 25 percent over ten years, and source its energy from local, renewable energy.

35

Put your money in a cooler place. If your bank continues to fund the expansion of fossil fuels and deforestation, you can move your money to a more climate-responsible institution. Be sure to tell your bank why you are closing your account. Look for a local not-for-profit credit union or a community development bank. Amalgamated Bank, for example, has pledged not to invest in fossil fuels.

36

Ensure environmental responsibility when you insure your property. Prospecting for oil and gas in remote locations is risky, so fossil fuel companies can't survive without insurance. But ironically, while insurance companies are often more than happy to provide coverage for fossil fuel extraction, they are in many cases decreasing their risk exposure in places that are experiencing the worst climate change impacts. The flooding coasts of Florida, the wildfire-ravaged counties of California—these are places where homeowners are finding it harder and much more expensive to insure their property. Write to or call your insurance company and point out that the irony isn't lost on you. If this argument falls on deaf ears, consider the new online homeowner and renter insurance company Lemonade. Lemonade is a certified B Corporation, with environmental well-being baked into its charter. The company has committed to never investing in fossil fuels.

37

Divest when you invest. Investing in both clean energy generation and the institutions moving toward renewables turns out to be profitable. "There is no longer a tradeoff between having a portfolio that generates competitive returns and one that invests in clean energy," David Cantor, principal and cofounder of New Mexico–based LongView Asset Management told me. This is true of some of the most basic investment modes out there. As of this writing, the S&P Global Clean Energy Index three-year return was 14.38 percent, compared to just 8.9 percent for the general S&P. In addition, a range of low-carbon mutual funds and exchange-traded funds (indicated by ticker symbols like LOWC and CARB) have boasted impressive returns over the last decade. These gains are likely to continue the more renewable energy generation declines in cost. And it's worth noting that as the cost of renewables continues to plunge, investors who put their money in fossil fuel companies run the risk that their money will become what's known as a "stranded asset"— money tied to resources buried in the ground in the form of oil and gas that is more expensive to access than power from competing renewables.

38

Stick it to the board. If you own any stocks in publicly traded companies—whether through a retirement plan, an investment manager, or otherwise—you can vote on any shareholder resolutions that make it onto a company's proxy statement ahead of its annual shareholder meeting. With increasing frequency, bank shareholders are putting forward climate-related resolutions. Vote yes on shareholder proposals that would force companies in which you invest to measure, disclose, and act on climate-related metrics. Shareholder activism has shown decidedly strong results of late. JP Morgan Chase voted to remove former Exxon-Mobil CEO Lee Raymond from the company's board after shareholders expressed dissatisfaction with Raymond's positions on climate change.

39

Invest in a "forever" forest. If at the end of the year you're looking to make charitable contributions to offset income, consider investing in a forest by donating to a land trust. Ecologists suggest finding a land trust in an area that you love that is trying to raise funds to acquire Forever Wild status for a local forest. This designation is important. Many land trusts will buy acreage only to turn it over to the state later. And many states have regular tree-harvesting as part of their state economic policies, even on protected lands. The Forever Wild specification means that trees will never be cut. More information about Forever Wild forests taking donations is included in the Resources section.

40

Reward transition. If we are going to truly change the energy economy of the country, we can't just build new carbon-free institutions from scratch and boycott the rest. We also have to speed the transition of existing emissions-intensive businesses to renewables. Investment professionals are devoting increasing attention to this transition. The firm Entelligent, for example, has developed a climate data platform that reveals that the speed at which a company transitions from fossil fuel dependence to renewable energy sources correlates with enhanced earnings and higher shareholder returns. To find which businesses are striving to transition and which ones are stalled out, investors can refer to the data of the nonprofit CDP (formerly the Carbon Disclosure Project). CDP grades companies from A to F on climate issues and releases data regularly via its website.

Fighting and Winning

Trimming your personal carbon emissions has two effects. The most immediate and obvious one is a simple raw reduction of pounds of CO_2 put into the atmosphere. The second and perhaps more important effect is that once we establish an effective climate diet for ourselves, we might work to get the nation on one as well. For those who are ready to participate in climate change advocacy, here are a few tips about how to maximize the impact of your actions. Just as replacing your fossil fuel–powered heater and air conditioner with a green electric heating and cooling system is vastly more potent than swapping out a traditional lightbulb with an LED, there are certain political actions we can take that are significantly more powerful than others.

41

Be specific. Politicians at any level of government tend to throw up their hands when their constituents demand that they "stop climate change" or "punish polluters." No single public official—be it a mayor, a governor, or a member of Congress—is capable of taking such broad, overarching action. Politicians are much more likely to respond to calls to action that can be accomplished within their given scope of authority and that are relevant to the people who voted them into office. A municipal composting bill, a state-level electric vehicle purchasing policy, a fight for access to safe tap water—these are all changes that politicians at their respective levels of government can realistically address.

42

Fight for racial justice while fighting for climate justice. "The very serious function of racism," the author Toni Morrison wrote, "is distraction. It keeps you from doing your work." This is immediately relevant to today's climate movement. Activists speak of this time as an "all hands on deck moment," with every person needed to transition our society away from fossil fuels. Racism keeps millions of American hands tied and unable to engage in that work. And this is work that is highly relevant to communities of color. As the marine scientist and policy advocate Ayana Elizabeth Johnson quite rightly points out, "People of color disproportionately bear climate impacts, from storms to heat waves to pollution. Fossil-fueled power plants and refineries are disproportionately located in black neighborhoods, leading to poor air quality."

43

Small and local adds up to big and national.
When we imagine where important policy decisions
are made, many of us think of Washington or perhaps our governor's office. But a multitude of impactful choices are made in town and city councils.
It's important, therefore, to vet and vote for climate
action candidates in your city or town. You can focus
on levers of change even closer to home. If you live in
a multifamily building, advocate for including utility and energy conservation measures in board resolutions. Similarly, if you have a child in school,
introduce climate measures to PTA and school board
meetings.

44

Educate when you demand. No one responds to a finger in the face. Help your elected officials and their staffs understand the matter at hand more fully. The reality is that most policy makers are not experts in everything. Use your deeper knowledge of a particular issue to help your elected officials feel more informed and capable of discussing the issue at hand with their fellow lawmakers.

45

Get personal. The best way to influence lawmakers is to visit them in person. Even if your politicians do not have an office in your hometown, staff will often arrange for temporary local offices that may be closer to where you live and allow specific windows of time for face-to-face engagement with constituents. If you can't visit in person, be personal in your correspondence. Petitions and form letters that you sign online are better than nothing, but the lawmakers I interviewed spoke repeatedly about the effectiveness of appeals that connect an issue to a real personal story.

46

Speak for the trees. As I've mentioned, healthy forests represent our greatest hope for removing CO_2 from the atmosphere. But tree-planting alone won't get the job done. Older and larger trees, already in the ground, accumulate carbon much more efficiently than new plantings. Forest ecologists, therefore, encourage something called "proforestation," a framework by which we protect older forests that already take lots of carbon out of the atmosphere. Typically, when trees hit 75 or 100 years of age, they enter their midlife growth spurt. From age 50 to 150 years, trees such as Eastern white pine go from storing around 20 tons of carbon per acre to over 70. Unfortunately, many states mandate the cutting of trees on state land once they reach this critical growth period. If you live in a municipality with public forest, you can lobby local politicians to remove or modify mandatory tree harvest laws. Public land is your land, too—you have a say in what happens to your trees.

47

Pay attention to what they do, not what they say. Many lawmakers running for office in conservative districts publicly underplay or refute the risk of climate change. But a few have a more climate-friendly stance when actually legislating. Conversely, many liberal politicians talk a big climate change game but in truth do very little about it. In the end, it's actions that matter. The League of Conservation Voters keeps an ongoing tally of all congressional votes on climate issues, and state offices keep similar records for state-level politicians. Check your lawmakers' actual votes and respond accordingly.

48

Donate strategically. Many candidates try to win our financial support by promising climate action. But when you make a small donation to an individual candidate, you have little leverage to make that candidate actually do something once in office. For this reason, some environmental organizations have set up campaign financing affiliates that make larger bulk donations, specifically supporting candidates who will keep up the climate fight once elected. You can donate to these action funds just as you would to a candidate's personal campaign fund. But while a lawmaker can easily ignore the $25 you throw into their kitty, it's much harder for that same lawmaker to brush off the demands of an entire climate justice organization that has just invested a five- or six-figure sum into their campaign. The NRDC Action Fund and the League of Conservation Voters' Action Fund are two campaign-financing instruments that offer this kind of donation opportunity.

49

Focus on the goal rather than the difficulties.
Publicly opposing business-as-usual with respect to climate change can open you up to trolling, social stigma, economic loss, and even physical violence. But just as civil rights activists had to endure police brutality to end the Jim Crow policies, the difficulties around the climate struggle can bring success and vindication. In July 2020 activists scored two major victories against the fossil fuel industry after suffering years of abuse. In one case, Duke Energy and Dominion Energy announced they would cease development of the Atlantic Coast natural-gas pipeline, a massive infrastructure project that would run natural gas under the Appalachian Trail. The same week, a federal court ruled in favor of the Standing Rock and Cheyenne River Sioux tribes, who had been fighting the Dakota Access Pipeline. The pipeline had already been built, but nevertheless the court said that its developer, Energy Transfer, had to

close it down and remove the oil it carried within thirty days. In a joint statement, the two companies said there was an "increasing legal uncertainty that overhangs large-scale energy and industrial infrastructure development in the United States. Until these issues are resolved, the ability to satisfy the country's energy needs will be significantly challenged." But what was really going on here was that activists persisted and persisted. Make no mistake, being difficult *is* difficult, but the payoff is a better climate for us all.

50

Make it for everybody. The very phrases "climate change" and "carbon footprint" are cultural signifiers that can cause a partisan backlash—this despite the fact that polling shows both Republican and Democratic support for climate action. Broadening the movement therefore requires strategic approaches to language. Appeal across the aisle to the universal pride we share in American innovation and economic strength. Solving climate change needn't be only a burden. It can be an opportunity.

Afterword

Can America really go on a climate diet? Can enough of us take the measures described above and refashion the way we live our lives and how our businesses and government relate to the planet? I would argue that we have done things just as dramatic before and that we can do such things again. In the fifty years between the first Earth Day and the fifty-first, we went from a nation where rivers burst into flame from pollution to one where water quality standards are some of the highest in the world. In that same period we reduced the six most significant air pollutants by as much as 77 percent. And for all my talk of the need to get more trees in American soil, in the last hundred years we've added

40 million acres of forest back to the American land-scape.

Our present dilemma is that fossil fuels are woven so deeply into the fabric of our society that we require not just a few industries to change their behavior (as was the case with many air pollutants in the 1970s); we need to change our very culture. With this in mind, here are a few final thoughts on how we can create a cultural environment that can speed the changes our planet so desperately needs:

Don't shame. Nobody is climate perfect. We are in the process of doing something that's never been done: building a society where we actually balance human needs with the survival requirements of the ecologies that support us. As we transition to that new and better future, encouragement of our less climate-enlightened friends and neighbors will prove a winning strategy far more often than smugness or condescension.

Don't blame the poor and powerless. It is extremely hard for people living paycheck-to-paycheck to consider policies that carry with them even the whiff of added financial cost. "Breakfast comes before ethics," as the early American conservationist Aldo Leopold put it. We must, therefore, argue as much as possible for policies that will both reduce economic inequality while also reducing emissions. In the spirit of the Green New Deal, which stresses job creation in tandem with regulation, we should always support efforts to add economic opportunity to climate initiatives as they arise.

Make your life your argument. As writers we're often told to "show, not tell"—that is, express in living action what we feel in our hearts. The same needs to apply to our striving toward a climate-balanced world. Enough with words. It is time to do. The sight of our actions in action is our best form of persuasion.

Acknowledgments

The principal challenge of writing *The Climate Diet* was distilling the deep thinking of so many individuals, each of whom has authored a body of work in their respective fields so extensive as to make the present effort feel like a mere paragraph. I must therefore thank my sources not only for granting me interviews and follow-up time but for working with me so that I might as concisely as possible render their thinking in a way that the lay reader will hopefully find approachable. In this respect, thanks to Gidon Eshel, Peter Tyedmers, Ray Hilborn, Ben Halpern, Arlin Wasserman, and Mary Grant for guiding me through the tricky work of arriving at fair estimations of the relative impacts of

Acknowledgments

different food and drink choices. In the arena of home energy and transportation, a similar debt of gratitude is owed to Pierre del Forge and Luke Tonachel of the Natural Resources Defense Council (NRDC) as well as Sidewalks Labs' Chris Edmonds and Solar One's Noah Ginsburg. David Cantor of LongView Asset Management and author Bill McKibben were key in helping me understand the way institutional investing and insurance affect the fortunes of energy companies. Also of critical importance in this regard was Alison Kirsch and the excellent *Banking on Climate Change* she coauthored for the Rainforest Action Network. In the political arena thanks to Vermont's Lieutenant Governor David Zuckerman and NRDC's Kit Kennedy.

In addition to specific interviewees consulted for this book, I'm also indebted to a not-small group of writers, teachers, friends, and family who reviewed the manuscript in different forms before it went to press. Foremost among them Carl Safina, Jennifer Jacquet, David Fanning, Neil Docherty, Sarah Spinks, David Gold, Katherine Baldwin, Harvey Greenberg, Sharon Messitte, and Hans Richter. Carolyn Hall, who compiled the tables and graphics for this book and fact-checked the working manuscript, was vital to the process. Thanks, too, to my editor Emily Cunningham at Penguin Press who saw the potential for a book in the nugget of an opinion essay, and to Clay Risen at the *New York Times* opinion page for commissioning that same nugget in the first place.

Lastly, much appreciation to The Safina Center, which has supported me as its writer in residence through many tumultuous economic years; and to my partner, Esther Drill, who has, book after book, borne a similar number of years of emotional turbulence.

Resources

Eating and Drinking

Tracking your food's carbon emissions impact: The Environmental Working Group's "Meat Eater's Guide to Climate Change and Health" is a comprehensive online resource that details the carbon costs of many different foods: meats, dairy, grains, and vegetables. This guide has useful and accessible information about the climate, environmental, and health impacts of your food choices, as well as easy-to-read graphics. See: ewg.org/meateatersguide.

For a more academic treatment of the subject, see Joseph Poore and Thomas Nemecek, (2018). "Reducing Food's Environmental Impacts through Producers and Consumers," *Science* 360, no. 6392 (June 2018):

987–92. science.sciencemag.org/content/360/6392/
987.

Food waste and compost solutions: The US Environmental Protection Agency has compiled a list of "Wasted Food Programs and Resources across the United States," which provides information about state and community efforts for recycling, pollution prevention, food rescue, food donation, and composting. See: epa.gov/sustainable-management-food/wasted-food-programs-and-resources-across-united-states.

Want to home compost but don't have outdoor space and need something clean and odorless for indoors? A Japanese DIY home-composting method requires just a cardboard box and a few additives that you can order online. The technique is described in: japantimes.co.jp/life/2020/06/28/food/how-to-compost-cardboard-box.

See also the article by Hiroko Tabuchi in *The New York Times* for instructions and results: nytimes.com/2020/05/06/climate/new-york-coronavirus-composting.html.

Safe tap water and water filters: How do you know the quality of your tap water? How can you choose the best water filter for your water? The nonprofit Food and Water Watch offers good guidance for reading water quality reports and choosing from various options for filtering your water at home and decreasing your dependence on bottled water. See: foodandwaterwatch.org/about/guide-safe-tap-water -and-water-filters.

Making Families

Plant a tree in someone's name: For every dollar donated, American Forests will plant a tree in a threatened wild ecosystem that has been designated a priority restoration project in the US. Donations on behalf of someone else come with a personalized certificate and a membership to American Forests. See: americanforests.org/ways-to-give/gift-of-trees.

Or, make a donation in a recipient's name to the Fruit Tree Planting Foundation. Fruit, nut, and medicinal trees and orchard training are donated to communities in need around the world. See: ftpf.org.

Contribute to a young person's college fund: Ugift is a service that allows family and friends to easily donate to a 529 college plan, a savings tool that holds funds in a trust for a student's education. You can purchase Ugift college contributions at ugift529 .com. And if there isn't a 529 in place for the individual in question, see the state-by-state plan guide to setting up 529s here: policygenius.com/blog/a-state -by-state-guide-to-529-plans.

Help out with a bike share membership: More and more cities around the United States (and the world) have established bike share programs and are expanding bike-friendly traffic rules and regulations. Know someone who would love to exercise and would like to be independent of mass transit or a car for local needs? Search for a program in your gift recipient's hometown and look for the option to purchase an e-gift certificate; if it's not offered, sign them up on the membership page. You can also refer to this report to see where shared bike and scooter programs exist in the United States: nacto.org /shared-micromobility-2018.

Give the gift of carbon offset: The United Nations offers a creative way to offset one's carbon footprint by investing the money value of *your* carbon emissions in a project that is working to reduce carbon emissions. Projects include efforts to supply solar water heaters, rapid transit systems, wind power, or clean cookstoves. The UN's step-by-step carbon emissions calculator allows you to base your gift on the recipient's household location and habits. See: offset.climateneutralnow.org.

Resources for parents of only children: *The Case for the Only Child* by Susan Newman is a frequently referenced book for weighing the pros and cons of having only one child. Dr. Newman debunks myths about only-child issues and presents facts and personal accounts to round out the experience of single childhood. This book can help support those discussing having only one child and gives valuable information to think about while making the decision. See: susannewmanphd.com/books/the-case-for-the-only-child.

One and Only by Lauren Sandler also debunks and investigates the thoughts around only children. Sandler addresses cultural assumptions and also, notably, the discussion around the societal costs, including climate-related ones, of having more than one child. See: simonandschuster.com/books/One-and-Only/Lauren-Sandler/9781451626964.

Exploring cohousing or communal parenting structures: This is very much an emerging concept, but Curbed published "Coming of Age in Cohousing," a good summary of some of the considerations of multiparent households, in 2019: curbed.com/2019/2/13/18194960/cohousing-families-communities-united-states-muir-commons.

Staying Home

Getting green power into your home: The easiest way to green your personal corner of the grid is to shop on the open market for an energy service company (ESCO) that can route renewable power directly to your home. Consumers can shop for an ESCO at green-e.org. In some states, you can choose an energy service company that can deliver power to your existing utility; in other states, you choose and pay a new company that controls the transaction.

Finding community solar in your area: If you want to power your home with solar energy but do not have a place to install solar panels, consider investing in a community solar project that allows individuals to purchase shares of a large, off-site, shared solar energy system. See the US Department of Energy's community solar guide to learn more: nrel.gov/state-local-tribal/community-solar.html.

The Interstate Renewable Energy Council's "Shared Renewables Scorecard" makes it easy to see which states had community solar projects as of the end of 2019 and how they were graded on their strengths and weaknesses: sharedrenewablesscorecard .org.

How a heat pump works: A heat pump collects and concentrates heat from its surrounding environment. That heat is then used to warm an indoor space or hot water in a tank. Since the electricity is used to move heat from place to place, it can also cool by reversing the process. More detailed descriptions of how the heat pumps work can be found at the Natural Resources Defense Council website: nrdc.org/experts /pierre-delforge/electric-heat-pumps-can-slash-emis sions-california-homes.

Guide to shopping for low-emissions appliances: One of the best ways to ensure that a new appliance will be energy efficient is to buy one with an Energy Star certification. This means the appliance has met the most recent US energy efficiency standards. At the Energy Star website, you can search by type of appliance and specify price range, brand, capacity, and more: energystar.gov/products.

To further help your selection process, the non-profit *Consumer Reports* has ranked their top energy-efficient choices for specific appliances, including refrigerators, dishwashers, and washing and drying machines.

Guide to programmable or "smart" thermostats: If you are considering changing your temperature control system to a "smart" thermostat—one that can automatically regulate your heat and cooling energy consumption—consult the "Smart Thermostat Guide" before diving in. From key points like knowing what voltage HVAC system you currently have to what tools are needed, this valuable checklist can help smooth your transition to more intelligent home climate control: smartthermostatguide.com/6-things-you-should-do-before-you-replace-your-current-thermostat-with-a-smart-thermostat.

Leaving Home

Gas mileage tips: The US Department of Energy has an excellent series of suggestions for shrinking your carbon footprint while driving. These include tips on driving efficiency, car maintenance, trip planning, and a report that ranks cars by gas mileage estimates: fueleconomy.gov/feg/drive.shtml.

Saving and Spending

Knowing your bank's record on fossil fuel financing: If you would like to find out how much your bank invests in fossil fuel companies, the Rainforest Action Network's 2020 *Banking on Climate Change* report is an extensive investigation into the top thirty-five international banking institutions that have heavily financed the fossil fuel industry over the last few years, complete with clear graphics, case studies, and various ways to explore the data: ran.org /bankingonclimatechange2020.

Climate-friendly investing: What investments are best for the planet's and your own future? You can get a better idea by consulting As You Sow, a share-holder advocacy organization whose goal is "to promote environmental and social corporate responsibility." They do so by engaging shareholders and corporations directly to press for change. For those looking to trade in their fossil fuel porfolio for a more environmentally and socially conscious one, As You Sow offers a ranked list of mutual funds and exchange traded funds (ETFs) that do not invest in fossil. The funds are graded with explanations and are easy to explore: fossilfreefunds.org.

Making forests "Forever Wild": If you know of a forest that should be protected from development, the Old-Growth Forest Network has a toolkit to walk you through the necessary steps to save it as a Forever Wild forest. Included on the site are sample legal documents, case studies, and comparisons of different protection measures one can pursue. See: oldgrowthforest.net/how-to-save-a-forest.

It is also worth noting that there are numerous local initiatives to declare forests as Forever Wild throughout the United States. Search your location and "Forever Wild" to see if efforts are already underway.

Fighting and Winning

Holding politicians accountable: The League of Conservation Voters "National Environmental Scorecard" on politicians and climate change is a record of how all members of Congress rank in terms of votes on environmental issues. These issues include everything from air, water, energy, forests, transportation, climate change, justice and democracy, and toxins to overall performance. Track your current (and prior) legislators' scores at scorecard.lcv.org/members-of-congress.

Notes

Introduction: Nothing or Something?

xii **disadvantaged communities that have already been disproportionately punished:** S. Nazrul Islam and John Winkel, "Climate Change and Social Inequality." United Nations, Department of Economic and Social Affairs. October 2017. DESA Working Paper No. 152S T/ESA /2017/DWP/ 152. un.org/esa/desa/papers/2017/wp152_2017.pdf (accessed July 14, 2020).

xiii **awareness of the problem has risen markedly:** A 2018 Yale University survey found "Seven in ten Americans (73%) think global warming is happening, an increase of ten percentage points since March 2015. Americans who think global warming is happening now outnumber those who think it isn't by more than a 5 to 1 ratio. Americans are also increasingly certain that global warming is happening—51% are 'extremely' or 'very' sure it is happening, an increase of 14 percentage

Notes

points since March 2015, matching the highest level since 2008. By contrast, far fewer—7%—are 'extremely' or 'very sure' global warming is not happening." A. Leiserowitz, E. Maibach, S. Rosenthal, J. Kotcher, M. Ballew, M. Goldbergand, and A. Gustafson, "Climate Change in the American Mind: December 2018." Yale University and George Mason University (New Haven, CT: Yale Program on Climate Change Communication, 2018). https://climatecommunication.yale.edu/publications/climate-change-in-the-american-mind-december-2018/2/

xiii **Per Capita CO$_2$ Emissions of the World's Leading Economies:** Hannah Ritchie and Max Roser, "CO$_2$ and Greenhouse Gas Emissions," 2017. Published online at ourworldindata.org.

xiv **most prodigious emitter of carbon dioxide:** China leads the world in *total* global emissions by far. But divide the number of tons of CO$_2$ emitted by China by the number of citizens of the People's Republic and the average per capita emissions is less than half of those in the United States. That said, there are worse per capita offenders out there than the United States. Saudis, Australians, and Canadians emit 19.28, 16.9, and 15.6 tons of CO$_2$ per person per year, respectively. But the United States is a huge country of 330 million people, an order of magnitude more populous than Saudi Arabia (34.2 million), Australia (25.5 million), and Canada (37 million). When you combine the United States' extremely high per capita emissions rate with its very large population you can only arrive at the conclusion: the United States is the nation most in need of a transformation.

xiv **global target for per capita emissions:** United Nations, Department of Economic and Social Affairs. "World Economic

Notes

and Social Survey 2011: The Great Green Technological Transformation," Chapter II: 27–66. E/2011/50/Rev. 1ST/ESA/333 (New York: United Nations, 2011). un.org/en/development/desa/policy/wess/wess_current/2011wess_chapter2.pdf (accessed July 13, 2020).

xv **a significant majority of Americans:** See Valerie Volcovici, "Americans Demand Climate Action (as Long as It Doesn't Cost Much): Reuters Poll," Sustainable Business, June 26, 2019. reuters.com/article/us-usa-election-climatechange/americans-demand-climate-action-reuters-poll-idUSKCN1TR15W, and Alec Tyson and Brian Kennedy, "Two-Thirds of Americans Think Government Should Do More on Climate Change," Pew Research Center, June 23, 2020. pewresearch.org/science/2020/06/23/two-thirds-of-americans-think-government-should-do-more-on-climate/ (accessed July 1, 2020).

xvii **anywhere from 2 to 8 percent:** Office of Energy Efficiency and Renewable Energy, "Fact #983: Proper Tire Pressure Saves Fuel." energy.gov/eere, June 26, 2017. energy.gov/eere/vehicles/articles/fact-983-june-26-2017-proper-tire-pressure-saves-fuel (accessed June 26, 2020).

Eating and Drinking

1 **carbon footprint of food:** Different analyses rank food differently or sometimes group food production together with other elements of the economy such as forestry. Calculation can also be complicated by the fact that transportation emissions costs, sometimes broken out as a category separate from agriculture, overlap with food production. The US EPA puts the total emissions impact of agriculture at 10 percent of

national US emissions. US EPA, "Sources of Greenhouse Gas Emissions." epa.gov/ghgemissions/sources-greenhouse-gas -emissions (accessed June 30, 2020).

2 **global soil stock:** Judith D. Schwartz, "Soil as Carbon Store-house: New Weapon in Climate Fight?" March 4, 2014. e360 .yale.edu/features/soil_as_carbon_storehouse_new_weapon _in_climate_fight (accessed June 30, 2020).

3 **Beef can cost the planet more than 27 kilograms:** Environmental Working Group, *Meat Eater's Guide to Climate Change and Health* (Washington, DC: Environmental Working Group, 2011). ewg.org/meateatersguide/a-meat-eaters-guide-to-climate-change -health-what-you-eat-matters/climate-and-environmental -impacts/ (accessed June 23, 2020).

3 **regardless of how cattle are raised:** Raising CO_2-intensive corn and soy to feed cattle is a major reason for the high emissions rating for beef; another is the destruction or repression of forests that would serve as carbon sinks were that land not forcibly kept in pasture. Still a third cause is the methane emitted by cattle burps—a gas that is 34 to 86 times more potent a greenhouse gas than CO_2, which, with the combined greenhouse gas emissions, actually makes beef an even worse culprit than lamb (J. Poore and T. Nemecek, "Reducing Food's Environmental Impacts through Producers and Consumers," Science 360, no. 6392 [June 2018]: 987–92). And while some have put forth the idea that grass-fed cattle can actually reduce CO_2 emissions, environmental physicist Gidon Eshel points out that the numbers just don't bear this out. True, grass-fed cattle don't rely on corn and soy for their forage. But those cattle munching on pasture that once was full of trees prevent those carbon-sequestering forests from regrowing, as

they would on land if it were left ungrazed. And even though grass-fed cattle in a well-tended pasture can, like the primeval bison herds that wandered the Great Plains, have some carbon-sequestration effect by pruning grass and promoting subsequent carbon-storing regrowth of those grasses, the density of modern grass-fed cattle operations ranges from one to three orders of magnitude greater than precolonial bison herds. That many cows on the land means that grasslands get effectively neutralized as carbon sinks.

Counterintuitively, the lowest-emissions beef out there is the hamburger you get in most fast-food restaurants. These industrial burgers tend to be made from "deaccessioned" dairy cows that no longer give milk. Since those animals deliver a double barrel of nutrition in the course of their lives in the form of both milk and meat, most adjudicators of carbon costs rate meat from killed dairy cows at about one-third the carbon cost of cattle raised exclusively for beef. For an overview of beef impacts, see R. T. Pierrehumbert and G. Eshel, "Climate Impact of Beef: An Analysis Considering Multiple Time Scales and Production Methods without Use of Global Warming Potentials." *IOP Publishing Ltd Environmental Research Letters* 10, no. 8 (August 2015). A discussion of relative impacts of different kinds of beef production can also be found at Poore et al., "Reducing Food's Environmental Impacts through Producers and Consumers." *Science* 360, 987–92 (June 2018).

3 **we literally piss it away:** Michael Tlusty and Peter Tyedmers, "Eat Too Much Protein, Piss Away Sustainability," Triple Pundit, November 23, 2015. triplepundit.com/2015/11/eat-much -protein-piss-away-sustainability/. See also Christopher L. Weber and H. Scott Matthews. "Food-Miles and the Relative

Notes

Climate Impacts of Food Choices in the United States." *Environmental Science & Technology* 42, no. 10 (2008): 3,508–13. doi.org/10.1021/es702969f.

5 **But if every beef-eating American switched to chicken:** C. D. Gardner, J. C. Hartle, R. D. Garrett, L. C. Offringa, and A. S. Wasserman. "Maximizing the Intersection of Human Health and the Health of the Environment with Regard to the Amount and Type of Protein Produced and Consumed in the United States." *Nutrition Reviews* 77, no. 4 (2019): 197–215. doi.org/10.1093/nutrit/nuy073 (accessed July 14, 2020), and personal correspondence with Arlin Wasserman, founder and managing director of Changing Tastes, changingtastes.net.

7 **Or the fish:** For a thorough analysis of the fuel costs of fishing, see Robert W. R. Parker and Peter H. Tyedmers, "Fuel Consumption of Global Fishing Fleets: Current Understanding and Knowledge Gaps," *Fish and Fisheries* 16, no. 4 (2015): 684–696. Interpreting the carbon cost of wild fisheries is complicated by the fact that different parts of the world have markedly different fuel efficiencies. Emissions costs are also strongly affected by which catch method is employed, and there are often several catch methods used for each kind of fish. Nevertheless, differences between types of fish remain relatively consistent from region to region. For the purposes of showing those differences clearly, I have used Tyedmers's and Parker's impressive and detailed data set and extracted data numbers only for North America and only for the catch methods most commonly employed to catch the kind of fish in question. Those looking to understand more subtle differences from region to region and catch method to catch method should consult the full Parker and Tyedmers publication.

Notes

7 **An average of all American wild-caught finfish:** "Carbon Emissions: Beef, Lamb, Lobster, or Fish?" *The Maritime Executive*. April 3, 2018. maritime-executive.com/article/carbon -emissions-beef-lamb-lobster-or-fish (accessed June 24, 2020).

8 **somewhere between chicken and pork:** Modern aquaculture has wide variation from country to country, but several sources put farmed salmon, tilapia, and catfish (the three most popular farmed fish in America) between 7 and 12 kilograms of emissions per kilogram of edible food. R. W. R. Parker, J. L. Blanchard, C. Gardner, et al., "Fuel Use and Greenhouse Gas Emissions of World Fisheries." *Nature Climate Change* 8 (2018): 333–37. doi.org/10.1038/s41558-018 -0117-x, and J. Z. Koehn and R. Hilborn, "Environmental Impacts of Nutrient Production in the Food System." PhD dissertation, University of Washington, 2020, portions submitted for publication as of the date of this writing.

8 **Fuel Used per Metric Ton of Fish Caught:** Robert W. R. Parker and Peter H. Tyedmers, "Fuel Consumption of Global Fishing Fleets: Current Understanding and Knowledge Gaps," *Fish and Fisheries* 16, no. 4 (2015): 684–696.

9 **shrimp, are notably terrible:** The nutrient-to-emissions ratio on shrimp noted also in J. Z. Koehn and R. Hilborn's "Environmental Impacts of Nutrient Production in the Food System."

9 **more than twice the CO_2 per acre:** P. Taillardat, D. A. Friess, and M. Lupascu, "Mangrove Blue Carbon Strategies for Climate Change Mitigation Are Most Effective at the National Scale," *Biology Letters* 14, no. 10 (2018): 251. doi.org /10.1098/rsbl.2018.0251. D. C. Donato, J. B. Kauffman, D. Murdiyarso, S. Kurnianto, M. Stidham, and M. Kanninen, "Mangroves among the Most Carbon-Rich Forests in the

Notes

Tropics." *Nature Geoscience* 4 (April 2011): 293–97. doi.org
/10.1038/ngeo1123.

10 **grand emissions champions of the animal kingdom:** Scottish Aquaculture Research Forum, Jonna Meyhoff Frey (preparer), "Carbon Footprint of Scottish Suspended Mussels and Intertidal Oysters" (2012), ISBN 9781907266447.

11 **a good vegan diet:** Seth Wynes and Kimberly A. Nicholas, "The Climate Mitigation Gap: Education and Government Recommendations Miss the Most Effective Individual Actions." *Environmental Research Letters* 12, no. 7 (2017). iopscience.iop.org/article/10.1088/1748-9326/aa7541/pdf.

11 **perfectly terrible citizen of the world:** Gidon Eshel, research professor of environmental physics at Bard College. Personal conversation, April 14, 2020.

12 **five times more emissions-intense:** Emma Newburger and Amelia Lucas, "Beyond Meat Uses Climate Change to Market Fake Meat Substitutes. Scientists Are Cautious," CNBC, September 2, 2019. cnbc.com/2019/09/02/beyond-meat-uses -climate-change-to-market-fake-meat-substitutes-scientists -are-cautious.html (accessed June 28, 2020).

14 **about 10 percent of most food's carbon burden:** Christopher L. Weber and H. Scott Matthews, "Food-Miles and the Relative Climate Impacts of Food Choices in the United States." *Environmental Science and Technology* 42, no. 10 (April 2008): 3,508–13.

15 **Roots rule:** Koehn and Hilborn as cited above suggest a range of emissions for different foods. In their estimations, roots and small pelagics have a range that is consistently lowest in emissions.

Notes

17 fifty times more carbon costly: J. I. Boye and Y. Arcand (eds.), *Green Technologies in Food Production and Processing* (New York, Springer: 2012), doi.org/10.1007/978-1-4614 -1587-9_9.

17 One study in the UK: S. J. James and C. James, "The Food Cold-Chain and Climate Change," *Food Research International* 43 (2010): 1947. doi.org/doi:10.1016/j.foodres.2010.02.001.

19 frozen foods typically have as much nutritional value: Linshan Li, Ronald B. Pegg, Ronald R. Eitenmiller, Ji-Yeon Chun, and Adrian L. Kerrihard, "Selected Nutrient Analyses of Fresh, Fresh-Stored, and Frozen Fruits and Vegetables." *Journal of Food Composition and Analysis* 59 (2017): 8–17. doi .org/10.1016/j.jfca.2017.02.002.

21 packaging accounts for around 5 percent: Hannah Ritchie, "Food Production Is Responsible for One-Quarter of the World's Greenhouse Gas Emissions" (2020). Published online at ourworldindata.org/food-choice-vs-eating-local (accessed July 13, 2020), J. Poore and T. Nemecek, 2018.

21 tremendous amount of electricity: Aluminum production is very energy expensive. In 2010, "the total world production of electrical energy was 20,261 billion kilowatt hours, meaning that more than 3% of the world's entire electrical supply went to extraction of aluminum." wordpress.mrreid.org /2011/07/15/electricity-consumption-in-the-production-of -aluminum/.

And this statement from the article below but sourced from the International Energy Agency 2010 report: "The production of new aluminum results in around 1% of global annual greenhouse gas (GHG) emissions. Mining, refining, smelting and casting primary aluminum releases about 0.4 billion tons (Gt) of carbon dioxide equivalent (CO_2e) emissions per year." climate.columbia.edu/files/2012/04/gncs-aluminum-fact sheet.pdf, Nico Tyabji and William Nelson, "Mitigating Emissions from Aluminum." The Global Network for Climate Solutions, Columbia Climate Center, Earth Institute, Columbia University.

23 **warming consequence dozens of times that of CO_2:** Rivka Galchen, "How South Korea Is Composting Its Way to Sustainability." *The New Yorker*, March 2, 2020. newyorker .com/magazine/2020/03/09/how-south-korea-is-composting -its-way-to-sustainability (accessed June 25, 2020).

25 **Putting lids on your pots:** Harold McGee, "The Invisible Ingredient in Every Kitchen," *The New York Times*, January 2, 2008. nytimes.com/2008/01/02/dining/02curi.html (accessed June 23, 2020).

25 **40 percent of the energy from the flame:** David Joachim and Andrew Schloss, "The Science of Cooktops." *Fine Cooking*, no. 120 (2012). finecooking.com/article/the-science-of-cooktops (accessed July 12, 2020).

25 **the majority of the toxic nitrogen oxides:** Pierre Delorge and Michele Knab Hasson, NRDC, "Gas Appliances Pollute Indoor and Outdoor Air, Study Shows," updated May 11, 2020. nrdc.org/experts/pierre-delforge/gas-appliances-pollute -indoor-and-outdoor-air-study-shows (accessed June 27, 2020), and David Roberts, "Gas Stoves Can Generate Unsafe Levels of Indoor Air Pollution," *Vox*, May 11, 2020. vox.com/energy -and-environment/2020/5/7/21247602/gas-stove-cooking -indoor-air-pollution-health-risks (accessed June 27, 2020).

Notes

27 **Drink from the tap:** Beverage Marketing Corporation (BMC), "Press Release: Bottled Water, the Largest Beverage in the U.S., Continues to Grow," May 29, 2019. beveragemarketing.com/news-detail.asp?id=558 (accessed June 28, 2020), Food and Water Watch, "Take Back the Tap: The Big Business Hustle of Bottled Water," February 2018. foodandwaterwatch.org/sites/default/files/rpt_1802_tbttbigwaterhustle-web.pdf (accessed June 28, 2020).

27 **A 2007 study found that making the billions of plastic bottles:** The Pacific Institute. "Integrity of Science: Bottled Water and Energy Factsheet: Getting to 17 Million Barrels." December 2007. Published online at pacinst.org/publication/bottled-water-fact-sheet/ (accessed August 4, 2020). See also Peter H. Gleick and H. S. Cooley, "Energy Implications of Bottled Water." *Environmental Research Letters* 4, no. 1 (2009): 014009.

27 **clean, safe drinking water for all:** For discussions on water supply equity, see ej4all.org/campaigns-and-activities/safe-water, and Watered Down Justice report from NRDC (September 2017), nrdc.org/sites/default/files/watered-down-justice-report.pdf.

Making Families

31 **25 percent of a flight's emissions:** Ugar Kesgin, "Aircraft Emissions at Turkish Airports," *Energy* 31, no. 2 (2006): 372–84.

33 **5 percent of the trees of the actual Amazon:** The estimate of a billion trees used per year to make boxes for online retail comes per Adele Peters, "Can Online Retail Solve Its Packaging Problem?" Fast Company, April 20, 2018. fastcompany.com /40560641/can-online-retail-solve-its-packaging-problem. By that reasoning, if we continue to use a billion trees a year for twenty years, we will have used twenty billion trees, the equivalent of 5.1 percent of the trees currently in the Amazon forest system.

35 **Carnivorous pets have big carbon footprints:** Gregory S. Okin, "Environmental Impacts of Food Consumption by Dogs and Cats." *Plos One* (2017). doi.org/10.1371/journal .pone.0181301 (accessed July 8, 2020).

Staying Home

42 **Average Cost of Energy in North America:** NRDC analysis of Lazard's Levelized Cost of Energy and Levelized Cost of Storage 2019. See Lazard, "Levelized Cost of Energy Analysis, Version 13.0," November 7, 2019, lazard.com/perspective/ lcoe2019. *Note: Gas refers to Gas Combined Cycle; Solar refers to Crystalline Utility Scale Solar PV; Wind refers to onshore wind.*

43 **build capacity for local power generation:** Noah Ginsburg, director, Here Comes Solar Program, Solar One. Personal conversation, April 21, 2020.

45 **natural gas is leaky:** Anthony J. Marchese and Dan Zimmerle. "The U.S. Natural Gas Industry Is Leaking Way More Methane Than Previously Thought. Here's Why That Matters." The Conversation, July 2, 2018. theconversation.com /the-us-natural-gas-industry-is-leaking-way-more-methane -than-previously-thought-heres-why-that-matters-98918 (accessed June 29, 2018).

Notes

46 more customers will almost certainly switch to electric: This observation was made by Pierre Del Forge, Senior Scientist, NRDC. Personal interview, April 14, 2020.

47 40 kilograms of carbon emissions per year: The Oak Ridge National Laboratory reported an annual savings of carbon emissions for 2009 residences of 4.757 Tg with a 1 degree Fahrenheit adjustment to home thermostats. In 2009, the US population was 307 million. Dividing those carbon savings by the population gives us a per-person savings of 15.5 kg carbon. An average household was 2.575 people, which makes the savings per home 40 kilograms of carbon per 1 degree Fahrenheit. T. J. Blasing and Dana Schroeder, "Energy, Carbon-Emission and Financial Savings from Thermostat Control." Oak Ridge National Laboratory, 2013. Report ORNL/TM-2013/55. US Department of Energy under contract no. DE-AC05-00OR22725. info.ornl.gov/sites/publica tions/files/Pub41328.pdf.

47 consider installing a relatively new electric-powered technology called a heat pump: "Costs and Benefits of Air Source Heat Pumps." Energysage. Updated September 27, 2019. energysage.com/clean-heating-cooling/air-source-heat -pumps/costs-and-benefits-air-source-heat-pumps/ (accessed August 4, 2020).

48 US Household Energy Use: US Energy Information Administration, Annual Energy Outlook 2020, Table 4, "Residential Sector Key Indicators and Consumption," eia.gov/outlooks /aeo/data/browser/#/?id=4-AEO2020&region=0-0&cases=re f2020&start=2018&end=2050&f=A&linechart=ref2020-d1 12119a.4-4-AEO2020&sourcekey=0 (accessed July 11, 2020).

Notes

53 **Kill the vampire:** Pierre Delforge, Lisa Schmidt, Steve Schmidt, and Pat Remick (eds.). "Home Idle Load: Devices Wasting Huge Amounts of Electricity When Not in Active Use." NRDC Issue Paper, May 2015, IP: 15-03-A. nrdc.org /sites/default/files/home-idle-load-IP.pdf (accessed June 29, 2020). In addition, note that some newer models have a "low power mode"; refer to your device's manual for how to access it.

55 **The fashion industry is responsible:** "How Much Do Our Wardrobes Cost to the Environment?" [sic] The World Bank online, September 23, 2019. worldbank.org/en/news/feature /2019/09/23/costo-moda-medio-ambiente (accessed August 4, 2020).

55 **emissions for a polyester shirt:** Deborah Drew and Gene-vieve Yehounme, "The Apparel Industry's Environmental Impact in 6 Graphics." World Resources Institute, July 25, 2017. wri.org/blog/2017/07/apparel-industrys-environmental -impact-6-graphics (accessed July 13, 2020).

55 **the second most energy-intensive appliance:** Noah Horow-itz, NRDC, "Call to Action: Make Clothes Dryers More Energy-Efficient to Save Consumers up to $4 Billion." June 12, 2014. Published online at nrdc.org/experts/noah-horowitz /call-action-make-clothes-dryers-more-energy-efficient-save -consumers-4-billion (accessed August 4, 2020).

57 **more than 2 billion acres are available:** After Russia, the United States has the second largest swath of reforestable land in the world—around 103 million hectares. Jean-Francois Bastin et al., "The Global Tree Restoration Potential." *Science* 365, no. 6448 (July 2019): 76–79. doi.org/10.1126/science .aax0848. It's also worth noting that other carbon sinks exist on residential properties. Seagrass beds, which can sequester

more than ten times the amount of CO_2 as terrestrial forests, are adversely affected by lawn fertilizers. Coastal property owners should therefore be particularly careful about lawn care. For more on seagrass, see smithsonianmag.com/science-nature/underwater-meadows-seagrass-could-be-ideal-carbon-sinks-180970686/.

58 **Just half an acre of lawn converted to forest:** C. Claiborne Ray, "Tree Power." *The New York Times*, December 3, 2012. nytimes.com/2012/12/04/science/how-many-pounds-of-carbon-dioxide-does-our-forest-absorb.html (accessed August 6, 2020). Quoting Timothy J. Fahey, professor of ecology in the department of natural resources at Cornell University, the article estimates an acre of mature forest will sequester 30,000 pounds of carbon and compares that to an EPA estimate of 11,000 pounds of carbon dioxide per year emitted by the average car. The article concludes that a full acre will sequester the equivalent of 2.7 cars per year. A half acre converted to forest should therefore equal a little more than one car's worth of emissions. Note these numbers can vary depending on tree species.

59 **Living in a freestanding house and driving are so emissions-expensive:** For a detailed and entertaining discussion of urban versus country living and their relative emissions impacts, see David Owen, *Green Metropolis: Why Living Smaller, Living Closer, and Driving Less Are the Keys to Sustainability* (New York: Riverhead Books, 2009).

Leaving Home

61 **76 percent of Americans drive to work alone every working day:** Richard Florida, "The Great Divide in How Americans Commute to Work," *Bloomberg*, January 22, 2019.

bloomberg.com/news/articles/2019-01-22/how-americans
-commute-to-work-in-maps (accessed July 1, 2020).

61 **commuting to work represents around 17 percent:** Using
2017 transportation emissions data from the EPA, transportation overall contributed 29 percent of the United States' total
carbon emissions. Light-duty vehicles (passenger cars, SUVs,
pickup trucks, minivans) made up 59 percent of the transportation emissions, so 59 percent of 29 percent = 17 percent of the
total. US EPA, "Fast Facts: US Transportation Sector Greenhouse Gas Emissions 1990–2017." Office of Transportation and Air Quality, EPA-420-F-19-047, June 2019. nepis
.epa.gov/Exe/ZyPDF.cgi?Dockey=P100WUHR.pdf (accessed
July 1, 2020).

62 **US Transportation Emissions by Vehicle Type:** US Environmental Protection Agency, "Fast Facts on Transportation
Greenhouse Gas Emissions," epa.gov/greenvehicles/fast-facts
-transportation-greenhouse-gas-emissions (accessed July 11,
2020).

63 **the CO_2 output of many individuals in the developing
world for an entire year:** Niko Kommenda, "How Your
Flight Emits as Much CO_2 as Many People Do in a Year." *The
Guardian*, July 19, 2019. theguardian.com/environment/ng
-interactive/2019/jul/19/carbon-calculator-how-taking-one
-flight-emits-as-much-as-many-people-do-in-a-year (accessed
July 1, 2020).

63 **about 8 percent of global greenhouse gas emissions:**
Manfred Lenzen, Ya-Yen Sun, Futu Faturay, Yuan-Peng Ting,
Arne Geschke, and Arunima Malik, "The Carbon Footprint
of Global Tourism." *Nature Climate Change* 8 (2018): 522–28.
nature.com/articles/s41558-018-0141-x (accessed July 1, 2020).

Notes

65 performing as fuel efficiently as possible: US Department of Energy, "Driving More Efficiently." fueleconomy.gov/feg /driveHabits.jsp (accessed July 1, 2020).

65 Engine idling accounts for 1.6 percent: Tom Jacobs, "American Idling: The Ecological Cost of Keeping the Engine Running." *Pacific Standard*, June 14, 2017. psmag.com/envi ronment/american-idling-ecological-engine-running-3771 (accessed July 1, 2020).

67 employees who switched to telecommuting: Nicholas Bloom, James Liang, John Roberts, and Zhichun Jenny Ying, "Does Working from Home Work? Evidence from a Chinese Experiment." NBER Working Paper no. 18871. March 2013. gsb.stanford.edu/faculty-research/working-papers/does -working-home-work-evidence-chinese-experiment.

71 business class seat has a huge carbon price: Duncan Clark, "Business Class Fliers Leave Far Larger Carbon Foot-print." *The Guardian*, February 17, 2010. theguardian.com /environment/blog/2010/feb/17/business-class-carbon -footprint (accessed July 10, 2020).

73 Prices for electric vehicles: Keith Barry, "New Long-Range, Affordable Electric Cars Coming Soon." *Consumer Reports*, April 3, 2019. consumerreports.org/hybrids-evs/new-long -range-affordable-electric-cars-coming-soon/ (accessed June 30, 2020), and Luke Tonachel, director, Clean Vehicles and Fuels Group, NRDC. Personal interview, May 4, 2020.

74 electric vehicle ownership is likely to save: Average American gas consumption is around 600 gallons per year (auto news.com/article/20150325/OEM06/150329911/average-u-s-gasoline-usage-lowest-in-3-decades-study-says) × average gas price of around $2.503 per gallon (statista.com/statistics /204740/retail-price-of-gasoline-in-the-united-states-since -1990/) × 10 years of vehicle ownership = $15,000. With an electric price equivalent of $1/gallon, that number is $6,000.

74 **known as vehicle-to-grid:** Elsa Wenzel, "Vehicle-to-Grid Technology Is Revving Up." Greenbiz. November 12, 2019. greenbiz.com/article/vehicle-grid-technology-revving (accessed August 7, 2020).

Saving and Spending

77 **save, borrow, invest, and insure:** Bill McKibben, "Money Is the Oxygen on Which the Fire of Global Warming Burns." *The New Yorker*, September 17, 2019. newyorker.com/news /daily-comment/money-is-the-oxygen-on-which-the-fire -of-global-warming-burns (accessed July 2, 2020).

78 **Banking on Climate Change:** Rainforest Action Network, BankTrack, Indigenous Environmental Network, Oil Change International, Reclaim Finance, and the Sierra Club, "Banking on Climate Change: Fossil Fuel Finance Report 2020." ran .org/bankingonclimatechange2020/ (accessed July 2, 2020).

81 **The college's students never gave up:** "The Key to Win- ning Victories against Big Oil? Perseverance." *The Guardian*, January 30, 2019. theguardian.com/commentisfree/2019/jan /30/the-key-to-winning-victories-against-big-oil-perseverance (accessed July 2, 2020).

85 **Ensure environmental responsibility:** Jaime Court, "Top 10 US Insurance Companies Invest $51 Billion in Fossil Fuels." Consumer Watchdog, October 9, 2018. consumerwatchdog .org/insurance/top-10-us-insurance-companies-invest-51

-billion-fossil-fuels (accessed July 2, 2020). See also Arthur Neslen, "Climate Change Could Make Insurance Too Expensive for Most People." *The Guardian*, March 21, 2019. theguardian.com/environment/2019/mar/21/climate-change -could-make-insurance-too-expensive-for-ordinary-people -report (accessed July 2, 2020).

89 **former ExxonMobil CEO Lee Raymond:** Bill McKibben, "Big Oil's Reign Is Finally Weakening." *The New Yorker*, May 7, 2020. newyorker.com/news/annals-of-a-warming-planet/big -oils-reign-is-finally-weakening (accessed June 30, 2020).

91 **Ecologists suggest finding:** The ecologists referenced here are Joan Maloof, professor emeritus at Salisbury University and founder of the Old-Growth Forest Network, and William Moomaw, professor emeritus of the International Environmental Policy at the Fletcher School, Tufts University.

Fighting and Winning

99 **Ayana Elizabeth Johnson:** "I'm a Black Climate Expert. Racism Derails Our Efforts to Save the Planet," *The Washington Post*, June 3, 2020. washingtonpost.com/outlook/2020 /06/03/im-black-climate-scientist-racism-derails-our-efforts -save-planet/ (accessed July 4, 2020).

107 **Forest ecologists, therefore, encourage proforestation:** Information in this section is drawn from an interview with William Moomaw, professor emeritus of the International Environmental Policy at the Fletcher School, Tufts University, April 10, 2020.

113 **two major victories against the fossil fuel industry:** Bill McKibben, "It's Been an Awful Week for the Fossil-Fuel In-

dustry," *The New Yorker*, July 8, 2020. newyorker.com/news
/annals-of-a-warming-planet/its-been-an-awful-week-for-the
-fossil-fuel-industry (accessed July 10, 2020).

Afterword

117 **as much as 77 percent:** Environmental Protection Agency,
"Our Nation's Air." gispub.epa.gov/air/trendsreport/2019/#high
lights (accessed July 4, 2020).